I AM POWERFUL, AND SO ARE YOU

Written By
Angela Adley

Illustrated By
Victor Onyenobi

Archway Publishing books may be ordered through booksellers or by contacting:

Archway Publishing
1663 Liberty Drive
Bloomington, IN 47403
www.archwaypublishing.com
844-669-3957

ISBN: 978-1-6657-3557-5 (sc)
ISBN: 978-1-6657-3558-2 (hc)
ISBN: 978-1-6657-3556-8 (e)

Print information available on the last page.

Archway Publishing rev. date: 08/30/2023

ARCHWAY
PUBLISHING

This book belongs to:

_____

Thank you, God, for purpose and direction.
This book is also dedicated to my
beautiful family and friends.
May you all continue to be, do, and have
all that God has in store for you!

Hi, boys and girls! My name is Angela.

I want to share something with you,
something you may not know yet.

You and I have superpowers!

Did you know that? Raise your
hand if you knew that.

Let's say it together: "I HAVE SUPERPOWERS!"

Yes! You have superpowers, lots of them!

YOU HAVE

SUPERPOWERS!

6

Who wants to know how to ACTIVATE and turn your superpowers on? Raise your hand if you do!

Well, friends. Your superpowers are voice-activated! These powers turn on when you first say the words: "I AM."

Next, you must DECIDE and then say ALOUD:

WHAT YOU WANT TO SEE

WHAT YOU WANT TO BE

WHAT YOU WANT TO DO

HOW YOU WANT TO FEEL

WHAT YOU WANT TO HAVE

DECIDE
WHAT YOU WANT!

12

Lastly, you must say the word "NOW" at the end of your "I AM" statement! Only a few simple steps! Easy, right?

After you DECIDE what those things are, you must SAY them ALOUD. As you IMAGINE those things in your MIND, write them down on paper. Then read them over and over while BELIEVING that WHAT YOU WANT HAS ALREADY HAPPENED.

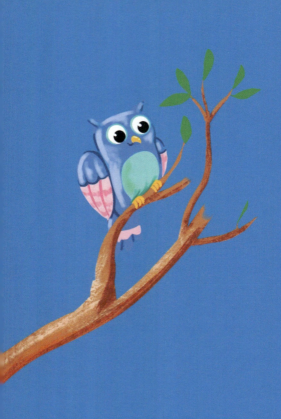

All right. Are you ready to play? Do you want
to try using your superpowers now?

DO YOU WANT TO TRY ?

18

Let's start with activating our power of SEEING! WHAT DO YOU WANT TO SEE?

I'll go first. I want to SEE CHILDREN AROUND THE WORLD ACTIVATING THEIR SUPERPOWERS NOW!

Now it's your turn! SAY WHAT YOU WANT TO SEE. As you say it three or four more times aloud, imagine HOW your body feels when you're SEEING WHAT YOU HAVE IMAGINED.

SEE WHAT YOU IMAGINE!

HOW DO YOU FEEL?

What emotions do you FEEL when you're SEEING WHAT YOU HAVE IMAGINED? As you go through your day, say and imagine these things over and over again!

Remember, write it down so you don't forget.

WHAT EMOTIONS DO YOU FEEL?

26

Let's keep going! Ready? Okay!
Now let's start activating our power of BEING!
WHAT DO YOU WANT TO BE?

I'll go first. I AM A BEST-SELLING CHILDREN'S BOOK AUTHOR NOW!

Now you try! SAY WHAT YOU WANT TO BE.

As you say it three or four more times aloud, imagine HOW your body feels when you're BEING WHAT YOU HAVE IMAGINED.

IMAGINE
WHAT YOU WANT
TO BE!

What emotions do you FEEL when you're
BEING WHAT YOU HAVE IMAGINED?

As you go through your day, say and imagine
these things over and over again!

Remember, write it down so you don't forget.

WHAT EMOTIONS DO YOU FEEL?

Are you tired? Let's keep going! Ready? Let's start activating our power of DOING!

WHAT DO YOU WANT TO DO?

I'll go first. I AM DOING SCHOOL VISITS AROUND THE WORLD, TEACHING CHILDREN ABOUT THEIR SUPERPOWERS NOW!

SCHOOL VISITS!

Now you try! SAY WHAT YOU WANT TO DO!

As you say it three or four more times aloud, imagine HOW your body feels when you're DOING WHAT YOU HAVE IMAGINED.

IMAGINE DOING WHAT YOU WANT TO DO!

HOW DO YOU FEEL?

What emotions do you FEEL when you're
DOING WHAT YOU HAVE IMAGINED?

As you go through your day, say and imagine
these things over and over again!

Remember, write it down so you don't forget.

WHAT EMOTIONS DO YOU FEEL?

Let's start with activating our power of FEELING! HOW DO YOU WANT TO FEEL?

I'll go first. I AM FEELING HAPPY AND EXCITED ABOUT CHILDREN ALL OVER THE WORLD LEARNING HOW TO ACTIVATE THEIR SUPERPOWERS NOW!

EXCITED CHILDREN!

Now you try! SAY HOW YOU WANT TO FEEL.
As you say it three or four more times aloud,
imagine HOW your body feels when you're
FEELING HOW YOU HAVE IMAGINED.

48

What emotions do you FEEL when you're FEELING HOW YOU HAVE IMAGINED? As you go through your day, say and imagine these things over and over again!

Remember, write it down so you don't forget.

WHAT EMOTIONS DO YOU FEEL?

50

Let's start activating our power of HAVING!
WHAT DO YOU WANT TO HAVE?

WHAT DO YOU WANT TO HAVE?

I'll go first. I AM HAVING A CHILDREN'S BOOK SERIES AVAILABLE FOR CHILDREN TO READ AND BE INSPIRED TO SHARE THE STORIES INSIDE OF THEM NOW!

CHILDREN
READIND AND BEING INSPIRED!

54

Now you try! SAY WHAT YOU WANT TO HAVE.
As you say it three or four more times aloud,
imagine HOW your body feels when you're
HAVING WHAT YOU HAVE IMAGINED.

IMAGINE WHAT YOU WANT TO HAVE!

HOW DO YOU FEEL?

What emotions do you FEEL when you're HAVING WHAT YOU HAVE IMAGINED? As you go through your day, say and imagine these things over and over again!

Remember, write it down so you don't forget.

WHAT EMOTIONS DO YOU FEEL?

Whoosh! That was a lot of POWER
we activated today!!!

A LOT OF POWER ACTIVATED!

Now YOU know the secret! YOU HAVE SUPERPOWERS! These SUPERPOWERS allow you to see, be, do, feel and have ALL that your heart desires!

NOW YOU KNOW THE SECRET!

Now go and tell all your friends how to activate their SUPERPOWERS! Until next time, use and activate your SUPERPOWERS every day!

Angela Adley is a pediatric speech-language pathologist residing in El Segundo, California. She's the author of the children's book, ***Growing Up without My Daddy,*** as well as a certified fatherless daughter advocate through Angela Carr Patterson's Journey to Being System. Additionally, Angela is a member of AAUW Beach Cities (CA) Branch, and a member of Understanding Principles for Better Living Church, founded by the late Reverend Dr. Della Reese-Lett.